EXECUTIVE EDITORS
Sarah Galbraith, Alan Doan,
Jenny Doan, David Mifsud

MANAGING EDITOR
Natalie Earnheart

CREATIVE DIRECTOR
Christine Ricks

PHOTOGRAPHER
BPD Studios

CONTRIBUTING PHOTOGRAPHERS
Katie Whitt, Jake Doan

VIDEOGRAPHER
Jake Doan

DESIGNER & TECHNICAL WRITER
Linda Johnson

PROJECT DESIGN TEAM
Natalie Earnheart, Jenny Doan,
Sarah Galbraith

AUTHOR OF PATCHWORK MURDER
Steve Westover

CONTRIBUTING COPY WRITERS
Katie Mifsud, Jenny Doan, Camille Maddox,
Natalie Earnheart, Christine Ricks, Alan
Doan, Sarah Galbraith

COPY EDITOR
Geoff Openshaw

CONTRIBUTING PIECERS
Jenny Doan, Natalie Earnheart,
Kelly McKenzie

CONTRIBUTING QUILTERS
Bernice Kelly, Deloris Burnett, Jamey Stone,
Betty Bates, Emma Jensen, Sherry Melton,
Cassie Martin, Amber Weeks, Sandi Gaunce,
Daniela Kirk, Amy Gertz, Patty St. John, Mari
Zullig, Megan Gilliam, Lauren Dorton, Sam
Earnheart, Mary Bontrager

CONTACT US
Missouri Star Quilt Co
114 N Davis
Hamilton, Mo. 64644
888-571-1122
info@missouriquiltco.com

content

Merry Christmas
from MSQC

December is filled with traditions. Some of them we've known since childhood and others we develop along the way as we grow older and establish our own lives. Each year, we look forward to these wonderful traditions: decorating, enjoying familiar foods, celebrating with family, and–my personal favorite–preparing gifts.

As quilters, we generally can't wait until the last minute to begin our gift making, which I think is great because it gets us thinking about our loved ones for much longer than just the month of December. It helps us keep the spirit of the holidays with us all year. There are few gifts that require as much of our time and thought as a handmade gift like a quilt, and I think that's pretty special.

During this holiday season, try not to get too stressed. Keep expectations manageable and set realistic goals for yourself. Pace yourself. Organize your time. Make a list and prioritize the most important activities. Remember the reason for the season. And when you are working on your quilted gifts, remember that finished is better than perfect!

In this season of giving, we want to take a moment to thank you for all you have given to our family. We wish you so much success and happiness in the coming year and we hope you have a very merry Christmas!

Jenny

JENNY DOAN
MISSOURI STAR QUILT CO

" We hope our magazine— BLOCK will inspire you to create beautiful quilts. "

'tis the *Season*

It's no secret my favorite time of year is from Thanksgiving to Christmas—the parties, the gift giving and the food! Oh, how I enjoy it all. I can finally bring out all my Christmas decorations in full force and fill the air with tempting scents of sweets—molasses-brown gingerbread, perfectly pink and red candy canes, oh and don't forget the chocolate! The tree fills my house with the intoxicating smell of pine and the fireplace burns golden with warm embers. Candles on the mantle and white lights on the tree twinkle like stars. Gifts are wrapped carefully with bright, cheery paper, tied up with bows, then tucked carefully under the tree. It's magical.

Quilting has also provided those magical experiences to my life this year. Being a part of Missouri Star Quilt Company and sharing this magazine with all of you has been the best party yet. We can't wait to jump into next year with all of you and create some more beautiful things. Merry Christmas from our team at Block magazine! Wishing you many magical moments this holiday season.

CHRISTINE RICKS
MSQC Creative Director, BLOCK MAGAZINE

SOLIDS

FBY8538 RJR Cotton Supreme Solids - Cream
SKU-9617-227

FBY1432 Moda Bella Solids - Robin's Egg
SKU-9900 85

FBY8513 RJR Cotton Supreme Solids - Candyland
SKU-9617-086

FBY8629 RJR Cotton Supreme Solids - Bordeaux
SKU-9617-082

FBY9391 RJR Cotton Supreme Solids - Silver
SKU-9617-125

FBY8623 RJR Cotton Supreme Solids - Navy
SKU-9617-030

PRINTS

FBY16359 Elementary - Vanilla Splash
by Sweetwater for Moda Fabrics
SKU-5560 14

FBY16363 Elementary - Splash
by Sweetwater for Moda Fabrics
SKU-5562 14

FBY18623 Hatbox - Cattail Cream
by Alexia Marcelle Abegg for Cotton+Steel
SKU-4002-001

FBY18115 Moon Shine - Camo Deluxe Strawberry
by Tula Pink for Free Spirit Fabrics
SKU- PWTP057.STRAW

FBY17928 Mimosa - Tumbling Boxes Charcoal
by Another Point of View for Windham Fabrics
SKU-39981-7

FBY17501 Glow - Quarter Moon Dusk
by Amy Butler for Rowan Fabrics
SKU-PWAB133.DUSKX

Charmed Spools

quilt designed by JENNY DOAN

I was at a quilt market a few years ago, chatting with others, when I mentioned how I couldn't get the idea out of my head to make a spool quilt. "Great minds think alike," I was told, "this year's market has six spool quilts!"

This spool quilt was inspired by my antique spool collection, something I keep to remind me of my heritage. You see, without some very talented seamstresses in my ancestry, I might not be here today.

My Grandma, Ingrid Olsen, was the youngest of thirteen children. Her older sisters left home and went ahead to America, finding work as seamstresses. I like to imagine that with every stitch, those brave girls dreamed of being able to help their parents, little brothers and sisters. They saved their money, sending it back to Sweden until there was enough to bring the rest of the family to join them in America.

When the time came, the rest of the family made their way to England where they tried to book passage on the Titanic. They were told that there wasn't room for them all and that they would be better off sending the men ahead of the rest of the family. But Ingrid's mother determined that the family was split up enough already, so they booked on a smaller ship where they could travel together. How grateful I am that my ancestors didn't board the ill-fated liner.

I will be forever grateful to my great-grandmother for keeping her family together, and of course to my great aunts who worked so hard sewing to bring our family here. You can see why both sewing and the symbol of the spool are very near to my heart.

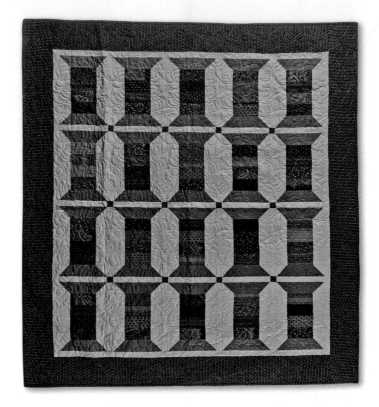

" I will be forever grateful to my great grandmother for keeping her family together . . . "

OUR ANCESTORS HAVE TAUGHT US MUCH ABOUT SACRIFICE, endurance, and love of family. We are so grateful to them for the fine examples that they are, and for the sacrifices they made so that we could have the blessings that we enjoy today.

Top right: Ingrid (the little girl in the dark sweater—Jenny's grandma) poses with her family on a dock.

Bottom right: Aunt Frida and Aunt Sigrid were two of the Sisters that came to America to pave the way for the rest of the family.

materials

makes a 58½" X 63" quilt

QUILT TOP
- (1) 5" square pack
- ¾ yd spool fabric solid
- 1¾ yds background/inner border solid
- 1 yd outer border

BINDING
- ½ yd coordinating fabric

BACKING
- 3¾ yds coordinating fabric

SAMPLE QUILT
- **Caswell County** by Jo Morton for Andover
- **Cotton Supreme Solids: Doll Face** (067) by RJR
- **Burlap Solids: Clay** by Benartex

1 pair up & sew

Sort the 5" squares by color into groups of 4. Each group of 4 similar colors will make 2 spools. Make 2 pairs from one group. With RST sew 2 seams on opposite sides of each pair. **1A**

Next, cut the pairs in half between the 2 seams. Mix and turn the pairs then sew them into (2) sets of 4. **1B** Repeat for all color groups.

Yield: 20 "thread sets"
Block size: 8½" x 5"

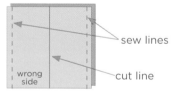

1A pair up RST and sew 2 seams on opposite sides; cut pairs in half down the middle between seams at 2½"

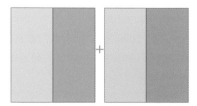

1B sew 2 pairs into a set of 4; make 20 thread sets

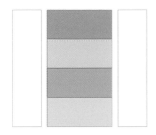

2 add background sections to either side of each thread set

3A stitch on the fold of the 2½" sections; note the angles

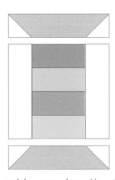

3B add a spool section to top & bottom of each thread set

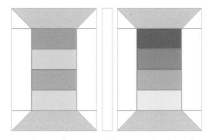

4A in each row a 12½" vertical sashing section connects one spool to the next

4B create horizontal sashing with (5) 9" sections & (4) 1½" squares; make 3

2 build the spool

From the background fabric cut (15) 2½" WOF strips. Subcut:

  (10) into (40) 8½" sections
  (5) into (80) 2½" squares

Add (2) 8½" background strips to either side of a thread set. Press to the background. Repeat for all thread sets.

Block size: 9" x 8½"

3 make spool ends

Cut (10) 2½" WOF strips from spool fabric. Subcut into (40) 9" squares.

Iron a diagonal crease in the 2½" background squares. Set 2 squares on the ends of the spool section as shown. **3A** Sew on the fold. Trim & press. Make 40.

Attach a spool section to top & bottom of each thread set. The narrow side of the "spool" should meet the "thread." **3B**

Block size: 9" x 12½"

Arrange the blocks into a 5 x 4 setting. Using a design board, floor space or a large table will help.

4 sashing

From the remaining background fabric cut (16) 1½" WOF strips. Subcut:

  (6) strips into (16) 12½" sections
  (4) strips into (15) 9" sections
  (6) set aside for inner border

From the outer border fabric, cut (1) 1½" WOF strip; subcut into (12) 1½" squares.

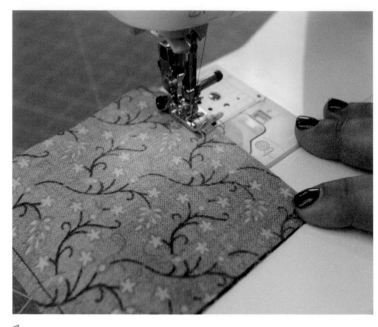

1 Sew a pair of 5" squares together with 2 parallel seams. See 1A.

2 Cut the pair in half between the 2 seams at 2½." See 1A.

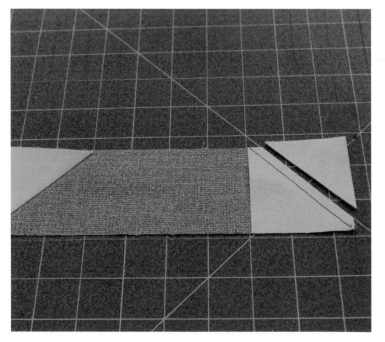

3 Add background sashing to either side of the "thread." Step 2.

4 Sew on the diagonal (top inside to bottom outside) for each side. Trim and press out. See 3A.

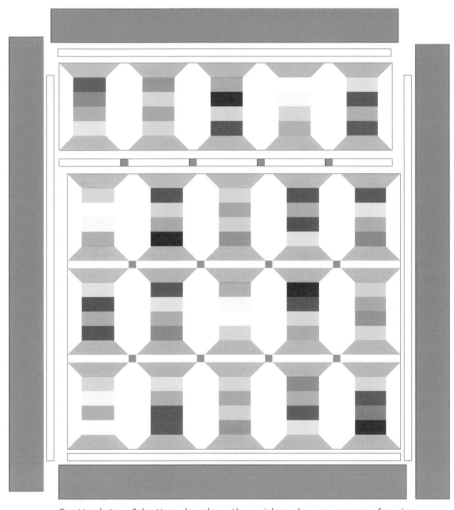

5 attach top & bottom borders, then sides; always measure for size

 For the tutorial and everything you need to make this quilt visit:
www.msqc.co/charmedspool

Build rows across first. Add (4) 12½" sashing sections to connect the 5 blocks of each row. **4A** Press to the sashing.

Make horizontal sashing. Use (5) 9" sections of background fabric and (4) 1½" squares. Sew squares between the 9" sections making a long strip. Press to the sashing, away from the cornerstones. **4B** Make 3.

Sew a horizontal sashing strip between rows to build the quilt center.

Quilt Center Size: 47" x 51½"

5 borders

Use the remaining (6) 1½" background strips for the inner border. Follow steps in *construction basics* to attach to the quilt. **A-D** Press to the borders.

Cut (6) 5" strips of outer border fabric. Attach to the quilt in the same manner as the inner border.

6 quilt & bind

Layer quilt top on batting and backing and quilt the way you like. Square up all raw edges.

Cut (7) 2½" strips from binding fabric to finish. See *construction basics* for greater detail.

Our
Missouri Star

quilt designed by NATALIE EARNHEART

When we moved our family from California to Missouri almost twenty years ago, we felt like we had moved to a different country. We came from a concrete jungle to farm country, and everything seemed new and different. We didn't speak the language (there's a town named Nevada here, but it's pronounced "Ne-VAY-dah"). Even the food was foreign (Gooey Butter Cake is not as weird as it sounds but just as fattening). We didn't even know how to heat our house!

Our new home in Missouri had a woodburning stove, something we had never used before. How hard can it be to warm up with a little fire? A lot harder than we thought, as it turned out! We sent our sons Al and Jake out to cut branches off trees to fill the stove, but, of course, when we tried to burn the fresh wood it smoked like crazy! We sat on the back porch until the smoke cleared, shivering and wondering how we got stuck with such a lemon of a stove. After laughing themselves silly, our neighbors finally took pity on us and brought over some seasoned wood.

Those neighbors ended up saving us from ourselves many times as we learned how to be Missourians. Even so, sometimes I insisted on learning the hard way. For example, during our first Christmas in Missouri, I told the neighbor, Ralph, about how excited I was to have my first real Missouri Cedar Christmas tree. My plan was to go out and find the perfect one on the day after Thanksgiving. Ralph tried to tell me what a terrible idea that was, but I thought he was just trying to spoil my plan. It took some convincing, but finally Ralph hitched up a trailer and drove us out to find my dream Christmas tree.

We brought that big beautiful tree into the house and decorated it and I don't know if I've ever seen a lovelier Christmas tree before or since. (And, of course, the house smelled like heaven.) So you can imagine my dismay when about four days later, I came downstairs and all the needles had dropped to the floor! There stood our once-glorious Christmas tree, now a stick covered with ornaments!

We had a good laugh and enjoyed our bare little Charlie Brown Christmas tree. Then as soon as Christmas was over, we went to the store and bought a fake tree! And I learned why real Missourians cut their Christmas trees down on December 24.

materials

makes a 75" X 98" quilt

QUILT TOP
- 1 print pack 10" squares
- 4 yds background solid
- ¾ yd outer border

BINDING
- ¾ yd coordinating fabric

BACKING
- 6 yds coordinating fabric

SAMPLE QUILT
- **Prisma Dyes** by Artisan Batiks
  for Robert Kaufman

- **Kona Cotton White** (1387)
  by Robert Kaufman

Note: Use a scant ¼" seam throughout

1 group fabrics

From the background solid fabric cut
WOF strips; cut into squares.

Cut (3) 10" WOF; (12) 10" squares
Cut (8) 7" WOF; (48) 7" squares
Cut (8) 6¼" WOF: (48) 6¼" squares

Select 3 prints and stack them with:
    (1) 10" squares
    (4) 7" squares
    (4) 6¼" squares.
    Make 12 stacks.

1 pair up RST

2 sew ¼" around outside edge
cut diagonally twice

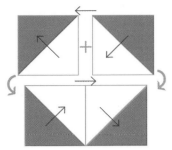

3 square-in-a-square; follow pressing arrows for more precise matching

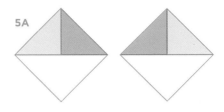

5A

5B a star leg unit; make 4

4A cut a pair of 10″ squares into fourths; sew the 5″ pairs together with 2 parallel seams

4B cut the pairs in half diagonally: 2 cut to the right & 2 cut to the left

4C yield: (8) quarter square triangles; 4 of each colorway

4D　　　**4E**

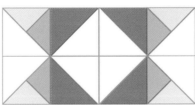

5C add 2 star leg units to the center block

5D sew 2 background squares to the ends of (2) star leg units

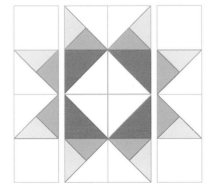

5E

2 make center HSTs

From (1) stack pair 1 solid and 1 print 10″ squares RST. Trim to 9½.″ Sew a ¼″ seam around the edge.

Cut across the squares diagonally twice. Try not to move the fabric as you make each cut. Sometimes this step is easier when using a rotating cutting mat.

Yield: 4 HSTs
Square up to 6¼.″

3 construct

Arrange the 4 HSTs into a square-in-a-square block with the background fabric facing toward the center. Follow the diagram.

Press the HST seams according the arrows for easier nesting and more precise piecing.

Join the top 2 HSTs together; then the bottom 2 HSTs. Press seams in opposite directions. Join top and bottom rows nesting seams to make the center block.

Block size: 12″ x 12″

4 make QSTs

From the same stack as above, pair (2) 10″ squares of print star leg fabrics RST. Make (4) 5″ pairs by cutting the pair in half once horizontally & once vertically.

Sew 2 parallel seams on 2 sides. **4A**

Cut them in half diagonally—2 from top left to bottom right; 2 from bottom left to top right. They must be opposite angles. **4B** Press seams to one side.

1 To make the quarter square triangles needed for the legs, sew the 5" pairs together with 2 parallel seams on opposite sides. See 4A.

2 Lay the 4 pairs on the mat with the same fabric facing up. Cut all in half diagonally: 2 from the bottom right to the upper left; 2 from the bottom left to the upper right. See 4B.

3 RST (right sides together) match the fingerpressed crease of the 7" background triangle to the middle seam of the QST. See 4D.

4 Sew them together along their long bottom edges. See 4E.

Yield: 8 QSTs (quarter square triangles); 4 of each colorway. **4C**

Cut the (4) 7" background squares in half diagonally. Find the center of the triangle's long edge by folding it in half. Fingerpress a crease. **4D**

RST match the fold of the background triangle to the seam of the QST. Sew them together along their long bottom edges. **4E** Square up to 6¼." Sort and stack QSTs by colorway.

5 star leg units

Select 2 QSTs—1 of each colorway. Turn them so their background fabric sides meet and the 2-color corners point up and toward the outside. **5A** Sew them together. Make 4 star leg units. **5B**

Block Size: 12" x 6¼"

Attach (2) units to opposite sides of the square-in-a-square block. **5C**

Use (4) 6¼" background squares to attach to either end of the remaining star leg units. **5D** Attach these units to the sides of the center block. **5E** Repeat steps 2-5 for each stack.

Yield: 12 stars
Block size: 23½" x 23½"

For the tutorial and everything you need to make this quilt visit:
www.msqc.co/missouristar

6 arrange & sew

Lay the 12 blocks into a 3 x 4 grid. Sew blocks into rows. Press seams to one side in even rows; to the opposite in odd rows. Sew all rows together.

Quilt center size: 69½" x 92½"

7 borders

From the outer border fabric cut (9) 3" strips. Follow steps in *construction basics*

to attach to the quilt. Press to the borders.

8 quilt & bind

Once you are finished with quilting, square up all raw edges.

Cut (9) 2½" strips from binding fabric to finish. See *construction basics* for greater detail.

patchwork *stockings*

designed by JENNY DOAN

Christmas stockings are a big deal in the Doan family. When the kids were small, I made a set of stockings modeled after the ones my siblings and I had used growing up. At that point, money was pretty tight and I wanted to be able to fill the stockings to overflowing, so I made sure to cut them a little on the small side. I chose a different Christmas print for each child but decorated all of the stockings with the same cute Christmas-themed appliqués. I loved to see those seven little stockings hanging in a row along the mantle each year.

When funds are low, you have to get creative with Christmas. Our stockings were never filled with candy or toys. They were filled with things the kids needed anyway: school supplies, new toothbrushes, even underwear! I'd wrap every single little gift separately so it felt like they were each getting lots and lots of goodies.

On Christmas Eve the stockings were filled and then hidden. When the kids woke up in the morning and came down to see

what Santa had brought, they would find only a clue in the spot where the stockings had been hanging. Then we'd all go on a treasure hunt to find the stockings. By the time they finally found the hiding spot, the kids were so filled with suspense they could hardly wait to empty their stockings and unwrap those pencils and socks!

Adding a little magic to Christmas doesn't have to be expensive. It's really all about creating a memorable experience. A fun presentation can make all the difference in making the holidays feel special. Over the years I have made several different sets of these stockings. Whenever our decor changed, I'd just whip up another set! They are a fun, easy way to add a personal, homemade touch to your Christmas celebration.

" Adding a little magic to Christmas doesn't have to be expensive. It's really all about creating a memorable experience. "

materials

makes a 12" x 17" stocking

MATERIALS

- (1) 5" square pack *(each stocking uses (10) 5" squares)*

BACKING, LINING, CUFF

- ½ yd coordinating fabric
  - **OR** 8" x 16½"—cuff
    (2) 14" x 18"—lining & backing

SAMPLE QUILT

- **Evergreen** by Kim Schaefer for Andover

1 making 4-patches

Pair up (10) 5" squares (5 pairs), 1 light, 1 dark. With right sides together (RST), sew (2) ¼" seams on opposite sides of the square.

Sew down one side of all the pairs, one after another and then back up the other side. Snip threads to cut apart.

Cut each pair in half between the two seams at 2½." Press to the dark fabric.

Mix the blocks up and sew them together end-to-end in one long strip, matching light to dark & nesting seams as you sew. Press.

Starting at the left, fold the first block over on top of the second RST. Cut at

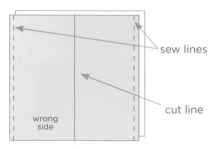

1A pair up RST and sew 2 opposite sides; cut pairs in half down the middle between seams @2½"

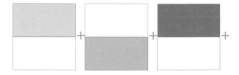

1B sew blocks together end-to-end; nest seams as you go

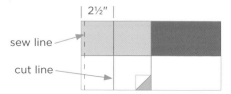

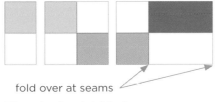

fold over at seams

1C make 4-patch blocks

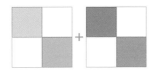

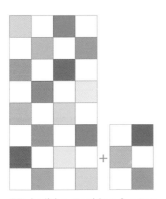

2A pair (2) 4-patch blocks 4X

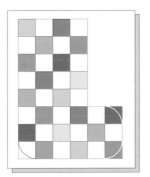

2B build a stocking & a toe section: 4 x 8 & 2 x 6

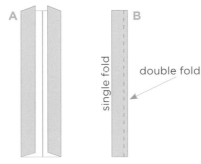

single fold

double fold

4A fold both sides to the center; fold closed
4B topstitch along double folded edge

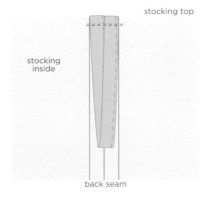

stocking top

stocking inside

back seam

4C attach the folded loop to the inside back seam

3A quilt the stocking; trim excess fabric & round off heel and toes

2½." You will have a 4-patch block and an extra 2-patch block. Continue folding and cutting the entire length of blocks.

Yield: (9) 4-patch blocks: 4½" x 4½"
(2) 2-patch blocks: 2½" x 4½"

2 create stocking

Sew (8) 4-patch blocks into (4) pairs making sure to stagger light & dark fabrics. **2A** Now assemble these into 4 rows and sew them together. Press (or re-press) seams to one side or the other in order to nest them as you go. **Setting:** 4 x 8

Match the last 4-patch and (1) 2-patch to create the toe section. **Setting:** 2 x 6 **2B**

Sew the toe section to the stocking with a short seam. The toe can be positioned on either side, it's up to you.

3 quilt & construct

Layer the stocking on top of batting and backing, both of which should measure about 14" x 18." Quilt or stitch-in-the-ditch as you wish. Trim around the entire stocking. Round off the toe and heel using a plate, jar or glass to help mark the curve. **3A**

Layer the stocking and backing RST and sew together with a ¼" seam. Start at the top and stitch down around the heel & toe and back up, leaving the top open. Backstitch at beginning and end. Trim off excess fabric. Clip curves and turn right side out.

1 Sew all the blocks together in one long strip. Fold over the first block on the far left at the seam. Cut at 2½". Voilà one 4-patch. See 1C.

2 Sew the toe section to the stocking on either side, it's your call! See 2B.

3 Layer the stocking on backing and batting. See 3A.

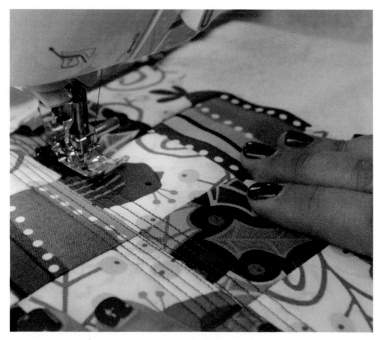

4 Quilt as desired. Step 3.

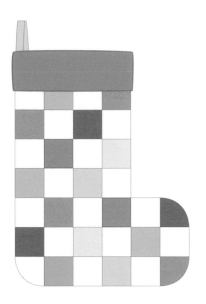

5 make a tube; fold it in half
WST matching raw edges

4 make a loop

Make a fabric loop to hang the stocking. Use a 1½″ x 5″ strip of extra fabric. Press in half lengthwise WST. Open flat and fold both long sides into the first crease. **4A** Press. Now refold the strip in half lengthwise enclosing the raw edges. Topstitch the double-folded edge. **4B**

Fold the loop in half. Position it inside the stocking on the back seam, loop pointing down. Its raw edges should line up with the stocking's raw edges. Double stitch across the loop at about ⅜″ from the top edge. **4C**

5 a cuff is nice

Use a rectangle (8″ x 16½″) of coordinating fabric. Sew the 8″ sides RST with a ¼″ seam, making a tube. Press the seam open. Fold the tube in half WST matching raw edges. Set the cuff inside the stocking folded edge down. Line up the seams in the back and all raw edges along the top. Sew a ½″ seam around.

Turn the cuff to the outside and pull up the loop. Your stocking is ready for Christmas!

 For the tutorial and everything you need to make this quilt visit: **www.msqc.co/ patchworkstocking**

31

foil-topped
ornaments

designed by JENNY DOAN

I love decorating for Christmas. All it takes to completely transform your home into a Christmas wonderland are a few twinkling lights and some carefully placed ornaments. There are few things as magical as gathering with the family next to the glow of a Christmas tree, soon-to-be-stuffed stockings hanging nearby above the hearth.

When I saw all of this year's new Christmas prints come in, my first thought was how I wanted to take the jelly rolls and make them into ornaments. My ornament pattern is so easy, but things really got fun when I discovered that if I ironed heat n' bond on aluminum foil, it could be used just like fabric! This "metallic fabric" makes perfect little toppers for my fabric ornaments. Every year I hang these ornaments all over the shops around town to get us in the Christmas mood.

Making homemade decorations and gifts is one of my favorite things about the holidays, but as our family grew, I found it increasingly difficult to keep up with my pastime. I noticed that I would spend the holidays stressing about finishing all my projects rather than enjoying them, so I decided it was time to make some changes. I settled on making one homemade gift for each of my kids' families, but provided an individual gift for each grandchild: I buy them one special Christmas ornament. Of course, I still want these gifts to be special and personal, so I take the time to

search for ornaments that really represent a hobby, talent, or accomplishment of each of the kids.

I never really knew if these ornaments meant anything to my grandchildren until I visited my daughter's home while she and her family were decorating their Christmas tree. I heard one of the kids say, "Mom, where is my special box of ornaments?" My ears perked up and I asked, "You have a special box of ornaments?" "Of course!" she replied, "All the ones you have given to me!"

One of my daughters even has a second Christmas tree just for her children's decorations. I love that they enjoy them and are excited every year to see what new ornament they will get. And when they are grown and have families (and Christmas trees) of their own, they will have this collection of ornaments that I hope will remind them just how special they are to Grandma!

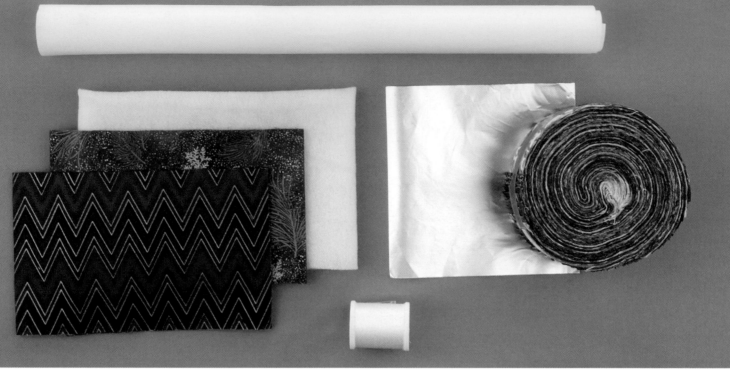

materials

makes a 6" - 8" ornament

Yields: 48 ornaments

PROJECT MATERIALS	NUMBER OF ORNAMENTS	
	5	50
2½" WOF strips	4	40 (1 roll)
Backing fabric	¼ yd	2¼ yds
fusible fleece	¼ yd	2¼ yds
aluminum foil 12" wide	30"	250"
Heat 'n Bond	½ yd	2¼ yds

SAMPLE ORNAMENTS
Holiday Flourish by Peggy Toole
for Robert Kaufman

1 sew

Sew (4) 2½" WOF strips together
lengthwise to make a strip set. To reduce
"bowing" sew in one direction and then
in the other as you add strips to the set.
Press seams gently to the same side.

1

2 cut

Use the Easy Circle Cut Ruler & the
18mm rotary cutter to make circles.
The 6" & 7" sizes work well. Subcut the
strip set into (5) 8½" squares. Fold the
squares in half. Align the ruler's guide
to the fold. Cut using the small rotary
cutter.

For each ornament, cut the same size
circle from background fabric.

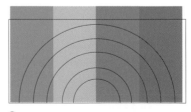

2

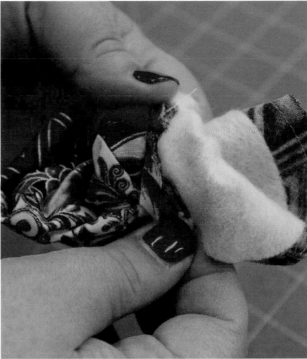

1 Right sides together sew the back (fusible fleece showing) to the ornament front. Backstitch at the beginning and end of a 3″ opening at the top. See 3B.

2 Clip curves and turn the ornament inside out. Push the seams out gently from the inside. Step 3.

3 Press the heat 'n bond to the dull side of the aluminum foil rectangle. Follow package instructions. Step 4.

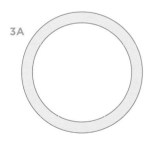
3A

3B

From fusible fleece cut circles one size smaller then the ornament size.

3 press & sew

Press the fusible fleece onto the wrong side of each backing circle. Follow package instructions for bonding. **3A**

Pair ornament front and back RST and sew around the perimeter with a ¼″ seam. Leave a 3″ opening for turning at the "top" of the ornament, backstitching at both sides. **3B**

Clip curves & turn inside out. Push the seams gently out from the inside to give the ornament its shape. Press. Set aside.

4 topper

Trace the topper shape provided on the next page onto paper. Cut around and use as a pattern or make a cardboard template.

For each ornament cut 6″ x 9″ rectangles from both Heat 'n Bond & aluminum foil. Iron the interfacing to the non-shiny side of foil.

Fold in half to 6" x 4½." Trace an ornament topper on the fusible side. You will be cutting out both sides of the topper at the same time. **4A** To make the hole in the hanger, fold the small circle in half & cut out a half circle. **4B**

Remove paper backing from the Heat 'n Bond.

5 attach topper

Sandwich the ornament between both sides of the topper covering the opening and press to seal.

Sew around the outline of the topper and add a ribbon for hanging through the hanger hole.

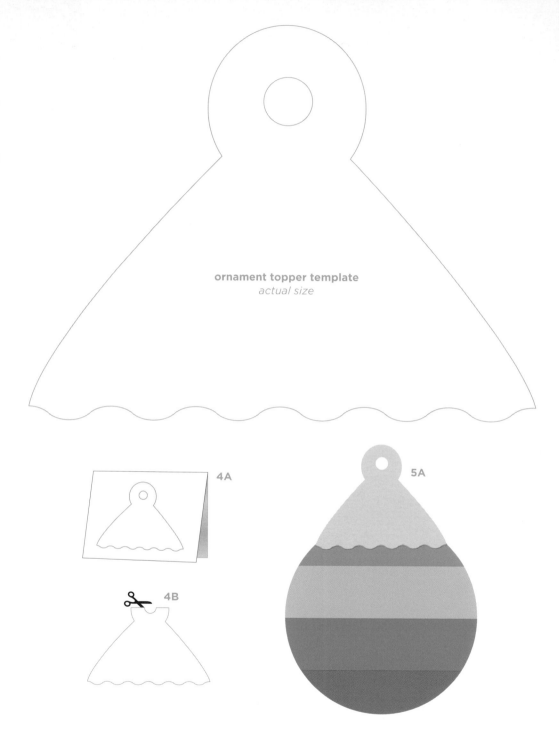

ornament topper template
actual size

4A

4B

5A

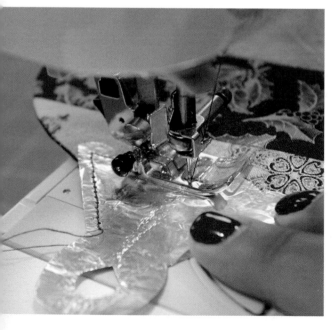

4 After pressing into position, stitch around the perimeter of the topper. Step 5.

 For the tutorial and everything you need to make this quilt visit:
www.msqc.co/foilornament

Dala Horse
runner

designed by JENNY DOAN

Food is an important part of our Christmas celebration. Our evening meal is typically a traditional Swedish smörgåsbord spread out on the table. The word smörgåsbord means "groaning board," and our table certainly does have reason to groan under the weight of all the wonderful Swedish food! Two of our favorite dishes to serve at Christmastime are Swedish meatballs and pepparkakor, a traditional ginger cookie similar to ginger snaps. The wonderful aroma of our holiday meal fills the whole house with Christmas-y goodness.

My maternal grandmother, or mormor, made the best Swedish meatballs but, like most grandmothers I know, she never used a recipe. I remember when I was a young mother my mormor came over to teach me and my daughters how to make her special meatballs. As she went along mixing and forming the balls, I wrote down every step as fast as I could so that we would finally have a recipe to replicate her delicious meatballs. Mormor made meatballs for the whole family every Christmas until she

was ninety-nine years old, and even though the rest of us have gotten pretty darn good at making those meatballs, they're just never quite as good as hers! Oh, how I miss her!

My pepparkakor cookie recipe also came from my mormor, but in this instance, I have the recipe card written out in her own handwriting! Pepparkakor cookies are rolled out very thin, cut into fun shapes, and baked until crisp. (Mormor was a make-do girl like me and I can

still picture her rolling out her cookie dough with a smooth drinking glass when she didn't have a rolling pin!)

Good food has the power to bring families together, and meals steeped in tradition enable even stronger family ties. As we crowd around our kitchen table, talking and laughing as we eat, our hearts are being knit together in a bond that can't be broken. And the real magic is, years from now, when the little ones are grown and the older ones are gone, just one sniff of our special Christmas smörgåsbord will be able to bring back a flood of memories of these happy times. How grateful I am for our Christmas dinners. They are really so much more than just food!

materials

makes a 17½" X 40" runner

PROJECT MATERIALS
- (6) 10" squares **OR** (6) 5" x 10" rectangles from scraps
- ½ yd outer border

SASHING/BINDING/BACKING
- 1½ yds coordinating fabric **OR** *different fabrics option:* ¼ yd sashing, ⅓ yd binding & 1½ yds backing

OTHER MATERIALS
- 12" x 12" square of red felt for appliqué **OR** 12" x 12" square of cotton fabric + Pellon Fusible interfacing
- freezer paper for tracing **OR** #659074 Sizzix Die
- glue stick optional

SAMPLE RUNNER
- **Snow Days** by Mitzi Powers for Benartex

1 cut

Cut (6) 5" x 10" rectangles from different holiday fabrics. Use your scraps or select fabrics from a pack of 10" squares.

From coordinating fabric* remove selvages & cut <u>lengthwise</u>:
  (3) 1½" LOF strips for sashing
  (3) 2½" LOF strips for binding
  (1) 26" x 48" backing
Subcut the 1½" sashing strips into:
  (7) 10" sections &
  (2) 34½" strips

If you choose to use different fabrics for sashing, backing & binding, see Step 6, page 4.

2 build the center

Rule of thumb: always press seams toward the sashing or borders.

Sew all large holiday rectangles together in a row along their 10" sides with sashing in between.

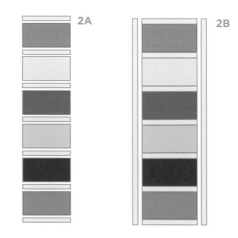

2A 2B

1 Cut the 10" squares of your selected fabrics in half once. Use (1) of the 5" x 10" rectangles of each fabric. Step 1.

2 Sew sashing strips between the rectangles along their 10" sides. Step 2.

3 The sequence: rectangle, sashing, rectangle, sashing. See 2A.

4 Sew the appliqués to the first & last rectangles of the runner with a buttonhole stitch either by hand or machine. Step 4.

Add the last (2) 10″ sashing sections to the beginning and end. Follow the diagram. **2A** Press.

Attach the 1½″ x 34½″ strips to either side. Press. **2B**

Quilt Center size: 12″ x 34½″

3 outer border

Cut (3) 3″ WOF strips from the outer border fabric. Subcut (2) strips to the width of the runner and attach one to either end. Press.

Measure the runner length and subcut 2 strips to that size. Attach to either side. Press. **3A** *No appliqué option:* skip to step 5.

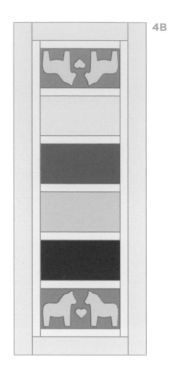

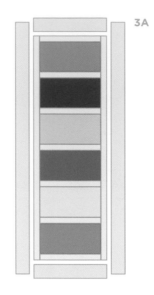

4 appliqué shapes

Use the Sizzix cutter and dala horse die to cut 4 horses from the felt. Temporarily position on the runner with glue stick.

Or, trace the horse shape provided onto the non-waxy side of freezer paper. Rough cut around the tracing, then iron to the felt, waxy side down. **4A** Cut along the traced line. Remove freezer paper by lightly heating with the iron. Reposition and cut again to make a total of 4 horses.

If you decide to use fabric instead of felt, fuse the Pellon interfacing to the back of the fabric first, then use the freezer paper method or Sizzix cutter to make the horses.

Iron (if using interfacing), pin or glue the appliqué shapes to the first & last blocks of the runner. **4B**

Make 2 hearts as well and position between the horses. Appliqué horses & hearts into place with a buttonhole stitch either by hand or machine.

5 quilt & bind

After layering on batting, and backing, quilt the runner the way you like. Square up.

Sew the (3) 2½″ LOF strips of binding together end-to-end with diagonal

seams. See *construction basics* for greater detail about binding.

6 additional notes

If you choose to use different fabrics for sashing, binding & backing (see materials list), cut:

    (4) 1½″ WOF strips of sashing
    (3) 2½″ WOF strips of binding
    (1) 26″ x 48″ rectangle for backing

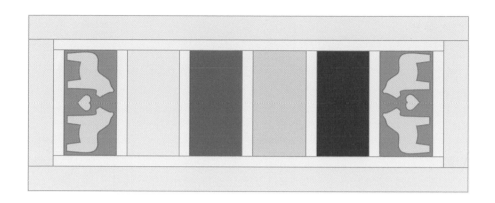

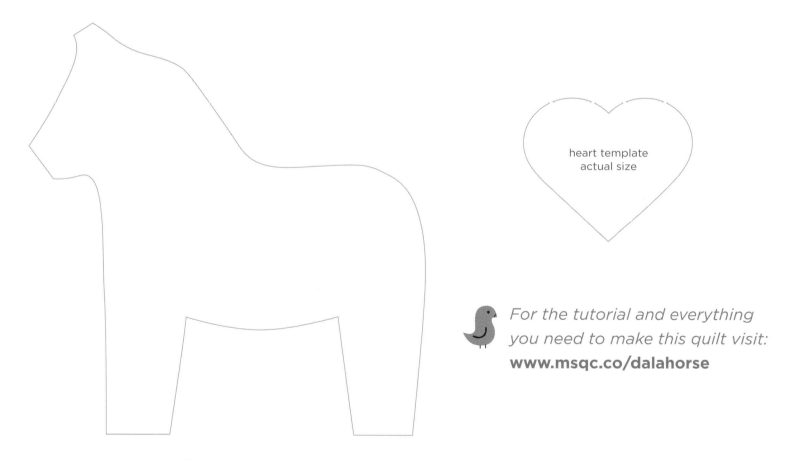

heart template
actual size

*For the tutorial and everything
you need to make this quilt visit:*
www.msqc.co/dalahorse

you can find this Sizzix template at: **www.missouriquiltco.com**
search for: **#659074 Sizzix Bigz Die - Dala Horse**

it's all an Illusion

quilt designed by JENNY DOAN

'Twas the night before Christmas, so cozy and pleasant, when kids started begging to open a present!

When the children were little, they regularly begged to open one Christmas present early. Eventually Ron and I would give in, but with the stipulation that the children had to open a present of our choosing, and, surprise, surprise, each and every year it was a new pair of Christmas pajamas! The kids pretended not to know what was inside, and they would squeeze and shake the boxes and make funny guesses about what it could be in order to keep up the ruse.

As a young mom, I loved to sew matching clothing for my children, and making Christmas pajamas was one of my very favorite projects. Every year, I had to start shopping early in order to find enough flannel for seven children and two adults. I remember one year in particular, I found yards and yards of navy and green plaid flannel. I made nightgowns for the girls and pants for the boys and on Christmas eve the nine of us looked fabulously festive in our matching pj's.

I continued to make Christmas pajamas every year for each of my children until they got married. (So my handsome bachelor Alan still gets a pair, haha!) But one year, after most of the kids had begun families of their own, I decided to bring back the Christmas pajama tradition. I set out to find enough matching flannel for twenty-one people and I made pajama pants and gowns of all sizes,

" As a young mom, I loved to sew matching clothing for my children, and making Christmas pajamas was one of my very favorite projects. "

from my towering boys down to the tiniest grandbaby. It was such fun having everyone together in their matching jammies, but, boy, twenty-one pairs of pajamas sure is a lot of work!

Today, we have reached twenty-one bodies with the grandchildren alone, not counting their parents! I don't even attempt to outfit the whole gang in Christmas pajamas anymore, but we have so many fun memories of all those Christmas Eves in our matching pajamas.

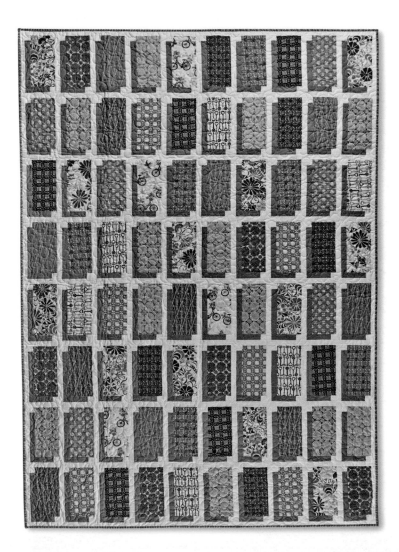

materials

makes a 67" X 94" quilt

QUILT TOP
- 1 pack 10" squares
- 1½ yds shadow solid
- 2¼ yds background solid

BINDING
- ¾ yd coordinating fabric

BACKING
- 5¾ yds coordinating fabric

SAMPLE QUILT
- **Artisan Batiks** by Lunn Studios for Robert Kaufman

- **Kona Cotton White** & **Gray** by Robert Kaufman

Shadow fabric		
Total: (30) 1½" WOF		
strips	subcut	number
20	9"	80
10	5"	80

Background fabric		
Total: (51) 1½" WOF		
strips	subcut	number
6	1½"	160
27	11"	80
14	7"	80
4	set aside	

1 cut

Cut (40) 10" squares in half.
Yield: (80) 5" x 10" rectangles.

Cut shadow & background fabrics according to the charts.

2 build the shadow

Add a 1½" background square to one end of all 9" & 5" shadow segments. **2A**

Chain piecing is a quick method of sewing elements together. Feed a square and a rectangle RST through the sewing machine with a ¼" seam. Continue sewing off the fabric a few stitches and feed the next strips through the machine

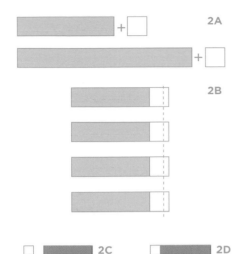

2A

2B

2C

2D

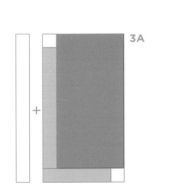

3A

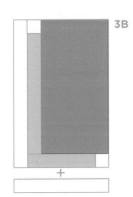

3B

and so on. **2B** Snip threads & press to the dark fabric.

Attach the longer shadow segment to the left of each block, white square at the top. **2C**

Attach the shorter segment to the bottom of the block, white square to the right. **2D**

3 add sashing

Begin with the 11" background segments. Attach them to the left side of the block. **3A**

Add the 7" segments to the bottom of the block. **3B**

Block size: 7" x 12"

4 arrange & sew

Lay out all the blocks in a 10 x 8 setting. Aim for a good overall mix of value and color.

Sew the blocks together across in rows. Press all seams in even rows to one side; in odd rows to the opposite side.

Sew rows together nesting seams as you go.

Tip: Press all seams toward the shadow & sashing segments.

5 finishing

Measure the length of the quilt center. Sew the last (4) 1½" background strips together end-to-end and cut to that length. Attach to the right-hand side of the quilt.

Measure the width and cut another strip to that size. Attach to the top edge. Press seams to the outside.

Quilt Center Size: 68" x 93½"

6 quilt & bind

Layer quilt top on batting and backing and quilt the way you like. Square up all raw edges.

Cut (8) 2½" strips from binding fabric to finish. See *construction basics* for greater detail.

1 A 1½" square is attached to one end of each "shadow" segment. See 2A.

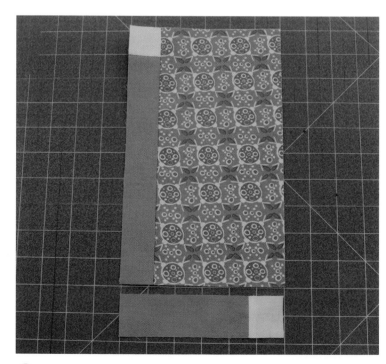

2 Sew the longer shadow section to the left of the rectangle, white square on top; then short shadow section to the bottom, white square to the right. See 2C & D

3 Repeat the same sequence but for background sashing: long section to the left; short section to the bottom. See 3A & B.

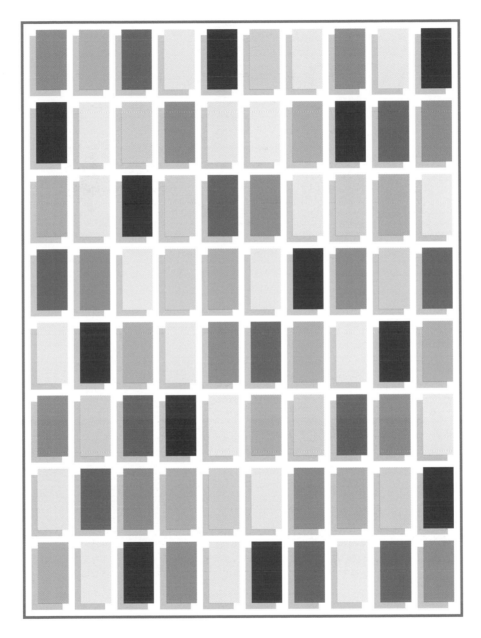

 For the tutorial and everything you need to make this quilt visit:

www.msqc.co/illusion

Hexagon Ornament
runner

designed by JENNY DOAN

When I was little, we always decorated the house for Christmas the day after Thanksgiving—not a day before! That was the official arrival of the season. We turned up the music and enjoyed all the memories that each decoration would bring! It was so moving to find the house transformed and realize that Christmas had come. Seeing the same familiar set of tomte gubbas on the shelf and Mom's delicate glass sprig of holly on the piano gave me a sweet, cozy feeling.

I still love the feeling of a home that's been decorated for Christmas. I can think of few things so warm and magical. I love how over time, as decorations become heirlooms, the memories that come along with them make your home a reminder of the love and fun your family has shared over the years.

One of my family's decorating traditions comes from my Swedish heritage. Just before we sit down to eat our Christmas dinner together, we all join hands in a big line and sing and dance around the Christmas tree and through

the house. You've never seen a family have more fun! We sing a traditional Scandinavian Christmas carol, "Nu är det jul igen," and even those who don't know the words sing out at the top of their lungs.

Originally, grandmother led the dance, then my mother did, and now I have the honor of carrying on the tradition. The beautiful light-studded Christmas tree, our beloved decorations, and this traditional Swedish dance and song make me feel connected to my family's past, present, and future. As I watch my cute grandkids giggle while they dance around the tree with me, I can imagine a Christmas day years from now when they will put Grandma's glass holly on their piano and dance around their own Christmas tree.

Pepparkakor Cookies

3/4 cup shortening	Cream shortening and sugar together. Add eggs and molasses. Blend well. Add the spices to flour and sift. Then add to creamed mixture. Let cool for 1 hour in fridge, covered with saran wrap. Then with a teaspoon scoop up dough and roll into a ball in your hands the size of a walnut. Have a bowl with sugar and roll ball in sugar. Put saran wrap over a smooth glass or mug. First put the balls on a slightly greased cookie sheet then flatten them with the glass. Put a plumped raisin or walnut half on the cookie. Bake at 350° 8-10 mins or until golden brown.
1 cup sugar	
4 T molasses	
1 egg beaten	
2 cups flour	
2 tsp. baking soda	
1 tsp. cinnamon, cloves, ginger	

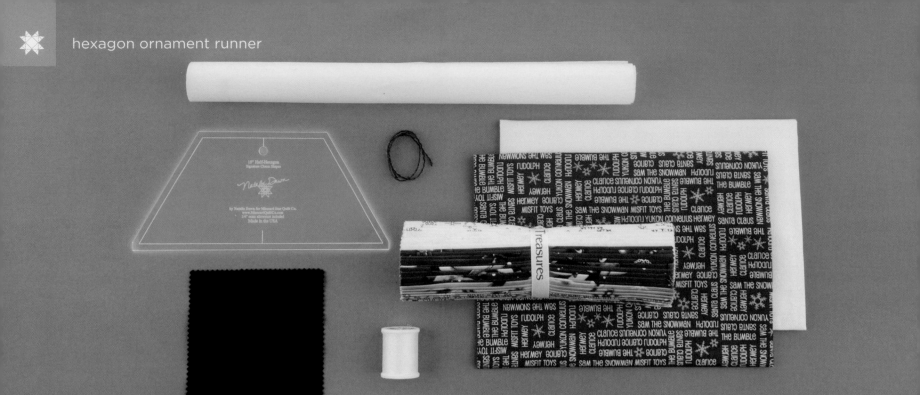

materials

makes a 19¼" x 37½" runner

MATERIALS

- MSQC 10" Hexagon Template
- 10" square Pellon Fusible interfacing
- ¼ yd tiny black rick-rack for hangers
- (6) 10" squares
- ¼ yd background/inner border
- ⅓ yd outer border

BINDING

- ¼ yd

BACKING

- ¾ yd coordinating fabric

SAMPLE QUILT

- **Rudolph** by Quilting Treasures

- **Cotton Supreme Solids Optical White** (033) by RJR

1 cut

With the MSQC hexagon template, cut out 6 shapes from (3) 10" squares: 2 from each. **1A**

Cut (3) 1½" strips from the background fabric. Set aside.

Keeping the background fabric folded, cut set-in pieces with a portion of the template. Set the narrow side of the template at least ½" into the fabric. **1B** Cut around. Make 12. **1C**

2 construct block

Attach 2 set-in pieces to each side of the hexagon. Match the set-in's narrow top to the wide bottom of

1A

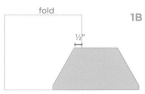

fold

½"

1B

1C

60

1 You can cut the 10" squares in half and double up the fabric to cut both out at the same time if you want. 1A

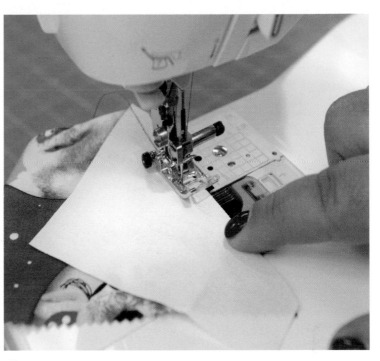

2 Attach set-in pieces to the slanted sides of each hexagon. See 2A.

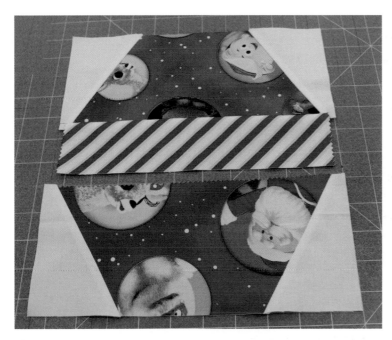

3 Use a 10" strip to connect the top and bottom portions of the ornaments, wide edges facing each other. Center all 3 elements. See 2C.

4 Trim the block to the 10" center strip. See 2D.

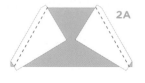

2A

2B

fingerpressed
creases aligned

2C

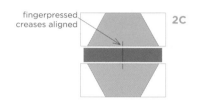

2D

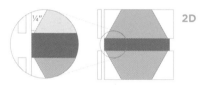

2E

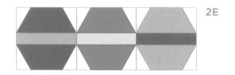

3A

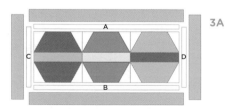

4A

1½" x 2½" topper

the hexagon. **2A** Sew RST along the angled edge. Press to the dark fabric. **2B**

Cut (3) 2½" strips from various 10" squares. Fingerpress the center. Fold each hexagon in half and fingerpress the center of its long, bottom edge. Sew a strip between 2 hexagons of the same print—bottom edges facing. **2C**

Trim the block's sides ¼" beyond the outer point of the hexagon. **2D**
Block size: 10"x 10¾"

3 borders

Measure the length of your runner & cut (2) segments to that size from the 1½" strips that were set aside. Attach to the sides. Always press to the borders. **A-B**

Repeat for the runner's ends, measuring the height. **C-D; 3A**

Cut (3) 3½" WOF strips of outer border fabric & attach in the same manner as the inner border.

4 ornament tops

Iron fusible pellon interfacing to the back of a 10" dark square of ornament hanger fabric. Cut (3) 1½" x 2½" rectangles. Snip off top corners at an angle. **4A** Sandwich a short rick-rack piece behind the ornament hanger top. Fuse into place on the runner. Sew around the topper with a blanket or zig-zag stitch to secure into place. Turn the rick-rack into the shape of a hanger. Stitch down.

5 quilt & bind

After layering on batting, and backing, quilt the way you like. Square up.

Cut (3) 2½" WOF strips for binding. Sew strips together end-to-end with diagonal seams. Trim & press seams open. Iron in half lengthwise WST. Attach to the quilt. Bring binding to the back and tack in place by hand or by machine.

 For the tutorial and everything you need to make this quilt visit: **www.msqc.co/ hexagonoranmentrunner**

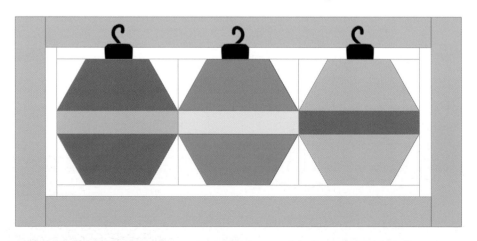

all wrapped UP

quilt designed by JENNY DOAN

When my parents became grandparents, they decided that they really wanted to help the family focus on the spiritual side of Christmas. They decided to begin a "walk in the woods" tradition for our family that has since become a cherished part of our Christmas celebration.

Every year as Christmas draws near, Dad goes out into the woods behind my parents' house and mows a path that twists and turns through the trees. No one is allowed to go back and peek at his preparations. He wants it to be a new and special experience for all of us. After he sets up the scene exactly as he wants, he gathers all of the kids and grandkids together.

Mom always has the house decorated beautifully, with twinkling lights and fragrant evergreen boughs, and as we wait, we chat excitedly with aunts, uncles, and cousins. But when the sun finally goes down, we grab our flashlights and walk out to the woods in silence.

It is so quiet and still out in those trees, and the moonlight shining through the bare branches adds a feeling of magic and mystery to everything it touches. At each turn in the path we discover some surprise: a small Christmas tree, decorated and sparkling, or a little gnome figurine holding a bucket of candy. We never know just what to expect around the next bend. Finally, we hear soft music playing in the distance, and as we get closer, we come upon one of the grandkids, whom Mom had asked to sing or play an instrument. Finally, upon rounding the last corner, we are greeted by two of the grandchildren

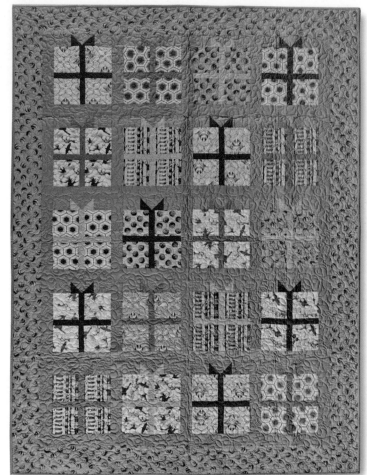

" . . . the moonlight shining through the bare branches adds a feeling of magic . . . "

dressed up as Joseph and Mary, standing next to the manger where our baby Jesus slept.

With this sweet little nativity scene before us and a shining star overhead, we all stand close together and sing every Christmas song we can think of. It is such a peaceful, lovely experience—the perfect tradition to remind us of the true meaning of Christmas.

Traditions are so important. They are the glue that binds our families together for generations. So whatever you celebrate at this time of year, don't hesitate to start a new tradition. They're what memories are made of!

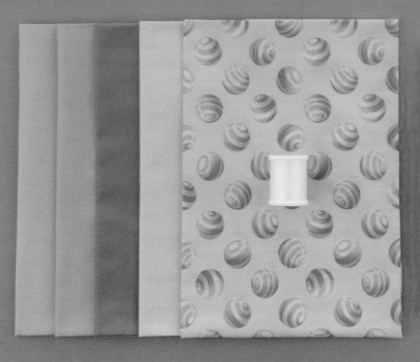

materials
makes a 61" X 81" quilt

QUILT TOP
- 2 packs 5" holiday fabrics
  (2x each print per pack) **OR** (1)
  10" square pack holiday fabrics
- 1¾ yds sashing solid
- 1¼ yds outer border
- (4) ¼ yd cuts for ribbon & bows

BINDING
- ⅝ yd coordinating fabric

BACKING
- 5 yds coordinating fabric **OR** 2 yds
  90" wide

SAMPLE QUILT
- **Bumble** by Tula Pink for Free Spirit
  Fabrics
- **Designer Solids - Gray** by Free Spirit
  Fabrics

1 select & cut
Organize squares according to
print and color. Make 20 stacks
that contain (4) 5" of the same
fabric. These are the "presents."

For the ribbon and bows cut each
¼ yd of fabric into:
Bows: (1) 2½" WOF strip;
    subcut into (10) 2½" squares
Ribbon: (3) 1½" WOF strips;
    subcut into (10) 5" segments &
    (5) 10½" segments

*If you are using 10" squares,
select 20 prints and cut each
into (4) 5" squares. Keep prints
together.*

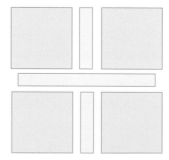

 TIP: *Connect the top and bottom rows by lining
up the 2 center ribbons. Visually they should
look like a single vertical ribbon.*

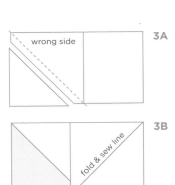

3A

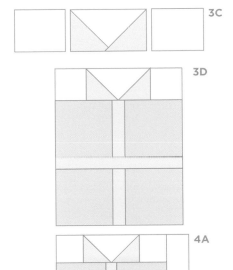

3B

3C

3D

4A

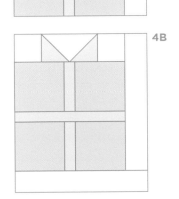

4B

2 build the block

Match a "present" stack with:
(1) 10½" & (2) 5" segments for its ribbon.

Add a 1½" x 5" strip between 2 squares—twice. Connect these with the (1) 10½" strip between them. Press to the ribbon. Make 20 presents.

Block size: 10½" x 10½"

3 make the bows

From the background solid cut:
(6) 2½" WOF strips; subcut into
    (20) 4½" segments &
    (40) 3½" segments

Fold (2) 2½" squares of "bow" fabric in half diagonally and iron a crease. This is a sewline. Position a square on one side of a 4½" background rectangle. Sew from bottom center to the upper outer corner. 3A Trim off excess and press open. Repeat for the other side. Mind the sewing angle! 3B

Next, add (2) 3½" rectangles to either side of the bow. Press to the bows. 3C Make 20 bow sections. Attach to the tops of the presents matching ribbon and bow fabrics. 3D

4 sashing

From the background solid cut: (14) 2½" WOF strips; subcut into (40) 12½" segments for sashing.

Add a 12½" segment to the right side of each present. 4A Chain piecing these will speed up the process. Always press to the sashing. Next add sashing to the bottom of each present. 4B Press.

Block size: 12½" x 14½"

5 arrange

Lay out the presents into a 4 x 5 setting. Sew presents together across in rows. Press seams in even rows to one side; in odd rows to the opposite side. Then sew rows together nesting seams as you go.

Cut (2) more 2½" WOF background strips. Sew them together end-to-end. Measure the length of the quilt center. Cut the strip to that size and attach to the left hand side to finish the sashing.

6 border

Cut (7) 5½" strips of outer border fabric. Follow steps in *construction basics* to attach to the quilt. Press to the borders.

7 quilt & bind

Layer quilt top on batting and backing and quilt the way you like. Square up all raw edges.

Cut (7) 2½" strips from binding fabric to finish. See *construction basics* for greater detail.

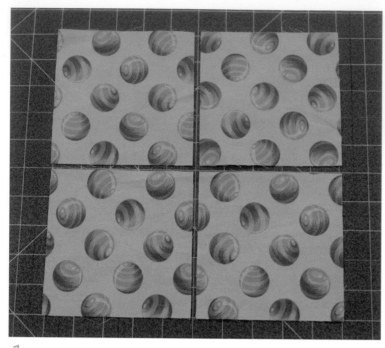

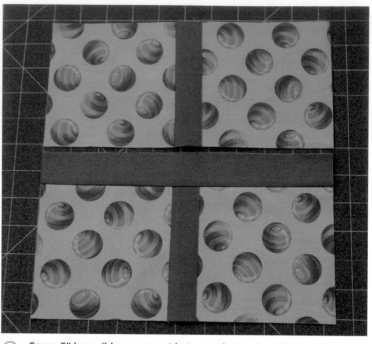

1 Every present consists of (4) 5" squares. See Step 1.

2 Sew a 5" long ribbon segment between the top 2 and bottom 2 squares. The 10½" ribbon segment connects the top & bottom rows.

3 The bow is a flying geese block. Once the 2½" square is sewn to the background fabric, trim off excess and press out. See 3A & B.

4 Attach (2) 3½" rectangles to either side of the bow. See 3C.

Quilt Center Size: 50½" x 70½"

 For the tutorial and everything you need to make this quilt visit:
www.msqc.co/allwrappedup

Dresden
placemats

designed by NATALIE EARNHEART

I love that special, magic feeling that only comes at Christmas time. When the kids were young, my husband and I tried to make our children's dreams come true on Christmas morning. We'd have each of the kids write up a list of the gifts they hoped to receive and then Ron and I would do our best to fulfill their wishes.

However, as the years went by we realized that at some point along the way, Christmas had become all about the presents. It wasn't about love; it became about how much money was spent on each child, or who had received more presents than the rest. This was not what we wanted for our family so we decided that we would not buy any presents the next Christmas. We still put up Christmas stockings, but other than that we made the rule that all gifts had to be handmade by the giver.

When we presented the idea of our homemade Christmas to the kids, they were not exactly thrilled. Nevertheless, they were willing to give it a try. I met with each of the kids from little five-year-old Josh up to the teenage girls and helped

them to come up with ideas. Over the next few weeks, our house became a little Santa's workshop as the children scurried about secretly preparing their presents. They were so excited to give their gifts, they could hardly wait for Christmas to come!

I'll never forget the first gift of that Christmas morning. Our sweet little Josh had made giant gingerbread cookies and decorated one specially for each person. He was so excited to give his gift and his brothers and sisters were gracious in receiving it, taking the time to notice the little details and appreciate all the work that went into making the cookies.

As each kid from youngest to oldest had a chance to hand out his or her gifts, there was a wonderful feeling of gratitude, and we all agreed that it was a very special Christmas. In fact, it was so much fun that we decided to continue the tradition of homemade Christmas indefinitely. The older the kids got, the more creative and clever they became with their gifts to one another. It was so exciting to see what fun ideas they could come up with every year. Focusing on creating something special for their siblings allowed the children to feel that joy that only comes when giving truly becomes better than receiving. Our homemade Christmases really helped us all to remember the real reason for Christmas.

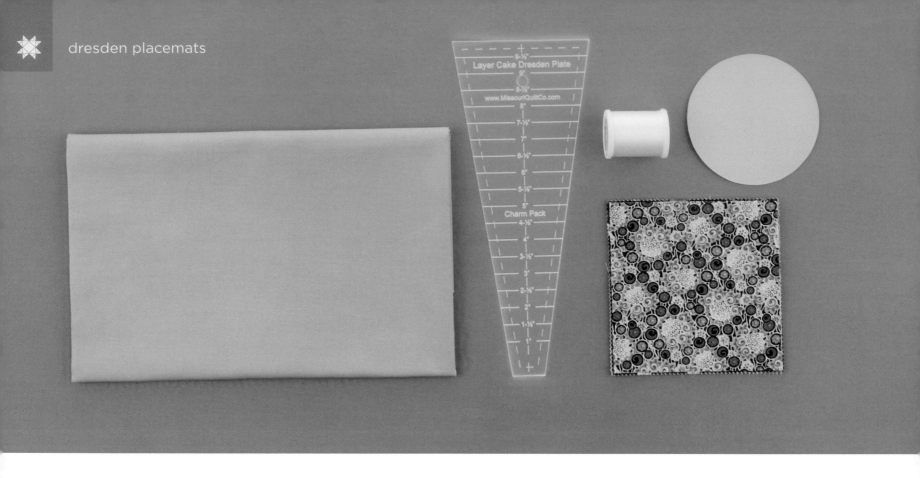

materials

makes (4) 23" X 15" placemats

PLACEMAT MATERIALS
- 2 packs of 5" squares
- ½ yd solid background

BINDING
- ¾ yd coordinating fabric

BACKING
- 1½ yds coordinating fabric
  cut into (4) 27" x 20" rectangles

SAMPLE QUILT
- **Downton Abbey: Lady Rose**
  by Kathy Hall for Andover Fabrics

- **Bella Solids Silver** (187)
  by Moda Fabrics

1 cut & sew

From the background fabric cut (4) 14½" squares.

Cut (28) 5" squares in half once.
Yield: (56) 2½" x 5" rectangles

Sew 7 rectangles together in a column along their 5" sides. Press seams in the same direction. Make 8. Attach 2 to opposites sides of each background square. Press toward the center. Set aside.

From (40) 5" squares, cut 2 wedges per square using the 5" mark on the ruler. Flip the ruler for the second wedge. **Yield:** (80) wedges

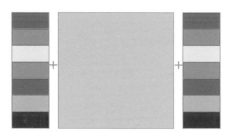

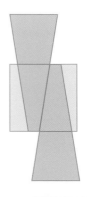

1 Fold the dresden shape in half lengthwise RST and sew across the wide top. Step 2.

2 Turn the folded corner right side out and center the seam in the back. Press. Step 2.

3 Sew 20 blades together side-by-side to form a circle. Step 3.

4 Prepare a circle center using a cardboard template and pulling a running stitch up around the shape. Press so the circle holds its shape. Remove the cardboard. Step 4.

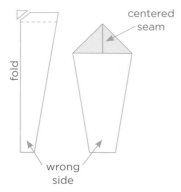

centered seam

fold

wrong side

2 fold wedges in half RST; sew across wide end; clip folded corner; turn & press

around leaving ⅜" allowance. Use a running stitch to sew around the perimeter. Place the cardboard template back inside and pull up the thread. Press the circle so it holds its shape, then remove the cardboard. Make 4. Set 1 into each plate center & pin.

Cut (10) 2½" WOF strips for binding. Use 2½ strips per placemat. Sew strips together with diagonal seams. Press seams open. Fold and press lengthwise WST. Attach to placemat. Bring folded edge of binding to the back and tack in place by hand or by machine.

2 create blades

Fold a wedge in half lengthwise RST. Sew across the top at the widest end. Clip the seam allowance 45° at the folded edge to reduce bulk. Turn the corner right side out, pushing the seam allowance to one side. Flip to the back. Center the seam down the middle creating a point. Press. Repeat for all wedges.

3 make a plate

Sew 20 blades together side-by-side using a ¼" seam. As each blade is added, they will naturally form a circle. Press seams to one side in the same direction.

4 plate center

Make a cardboard circle about 3½"-4" diameter using a bowl or mug. Make sure it covers the center. Use this as a template. Trace a circle onto a 5" fabric square. Cut

5 finishing

Center a dresden plate onto each pre-pared placemat. Pin into place.

Appliqué all the elements into place by hand or machine. A blanket, straight or zig-zag stitch is recommended for machine appliqué.

Layer each placemat onto backing and batting. Quilt. Square up.

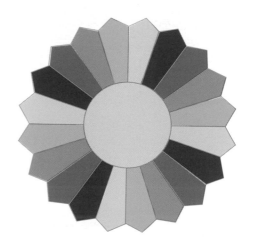

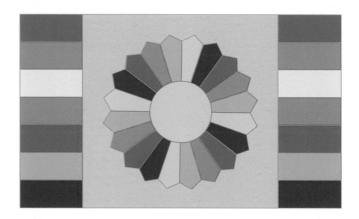

For the tutorial and everything you need to make this quilt visit:
www.msqc.co/dresdenplacemats

two table toppers

designed by JENNY DOAN

Our family's Swedish heritage is never more apparent than at the holidays. For us, the Christmas holiday begins on December 13, Santa Lucia Day. Early in the morning when it is still dark outside, the oldest girl in the house gets up while everyone is sleeping and makes traditional Santa Lucia buns and hot chocolate. She then dresses like Santa Lucia, in a long white gown with a red sash and with a wreath full of lit candles on her head, and wakes each family member with a bun and a cup of cocoa. It is a magical thing when that child dressed in white enters a dark room by candlelight and whispers, "Happy Santa Lucia Day."

Of course, that is the way it is supposed to happen, and usually at our house it was just like that, but there was that one year that things went a little differently...

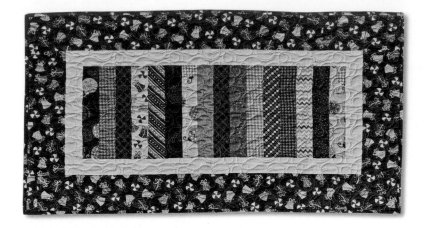

That year our daughter Sarah thought her grandmother would love a surprise visit from Santa Lucia. She drove over to my mother's house in the dark and quietly delivered her special holiday breakfast. Sarah looked beautiful in her traditional costume and my mother was so surprised.

Sarah felt so great about bringing some warmth and light to her mormor's day that she could feel it in her heart . . . and in her car. You see, she was so distracted with the loveliness of the morning that she had forgotten she was wearing burning candles on her head and lit the roof of her car on fire!

Santa Lucia
English translation

Night walks with a heavy step
Round yard and hearth,
As the sun departs from earth,
Shadows are brooding.
There in our dark house,
Walking with lit candles,
Santa Lucia, Santa Lucia!

Night walks grand, yet silent,
Now hear its gentle wings,
In every room so hushed,
Whispering like wings.
Look, at our threshold stands,
White-clad with light in her hair,
Santa Lucia, Santa Lucia!

Darkness shall take flight soon,
From earth's valleys.
So she speaks
Wonderful words to us:
A new day will rise again
From the rosy sky...
Santa Lucia, Santa Lucia!

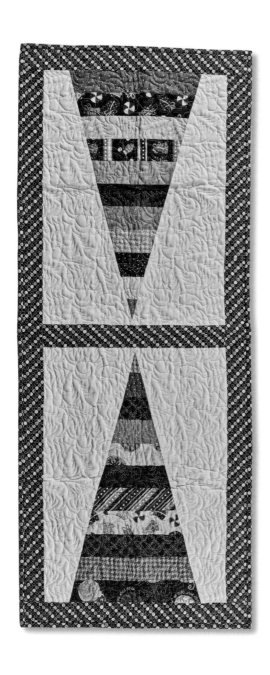

materials

makes a 23½" x 44" table topper

MATERIALS
- (1) 2½" WOF print roll
- ¼ yd inner border
- ½ yd outer border

BACKING & BINDING
- 1½ yds coordinating fabric (*Note: cutting done length of fabric*)

SAMPLE QUILT
- **Merry & Bright** by Kimberbell Designs for Maywood Studios

- **Cotton Supreme Solids Optical White** (033) by RJR

1 make the center

Choose 16 jelly roll strips from a holiday fabric collection. Select a mixture of colors and values. Cut a 14" segment from each strip. Sew these together lengthwise. **1A** *See Tip.* Press all seams to the same side.

Square up one side of the strip's ends removing all selvages.

Trim to 12" making a striped rectangle. **1B**

Table Runner Center: 12" x 32½"

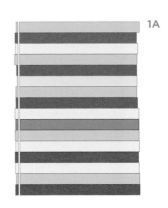

1A

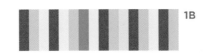

1B

2 borders

Cut (3) 2½" strips of inner border fabric.

Measure the entire length. Subcut (2) strips to that size and attach to the long sides of the runner. Always press to the borders.

Measure the width and subcut (2) sections that size from the last strip. Sew to the short sides. 2A

Repeat for the outer borders, cutting (4) 4" strips of outer border fabric. 2B

3 quilt & bind

From the background/binding fabric remove selvages & cut (3) 2½" LOF strips for binding. Sew the strips end-to-end with diagonal seams. Press seams open. Iron in half lengthwise WST. Set aside.

Use the remaining fabric for backing (32" x 54"). After layering the runner on batting and backing, quilt the way you like. Square up.

Now attach the binding to the quilt edge. Bring binding to the back and tack in place by hand or by machine. *See binding tutorial for more detail on pages 100-101.*

 TIP: *To reduce "arcing" of the strips, piece them together by first sewing in one direction; then sewing the next strip in the opposite direction. Continue in this manner. Gently press the seams using a cotton setting with steam. Avoid pushing them out of shape.*

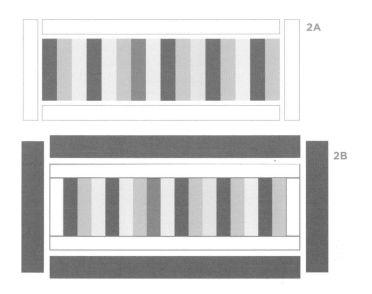

2A

2B

 For the tutorial and everything you need to make this quilt visit:
www.msqc.co/candylandrunner

materials

makes a 18" x 47" table topper

MATERIALS

- (1) 2½" WOF print roll
- ½ yd background solid

BORDER, BACKING & BINDING (BBB)

- 1½ yds coordinating fabric

SAMPLE QUILT

- **Merry & Bright** by Kimberbell Designs for Maywood Studios

- **Cotton Supreme Solids Optical White** (033) by RJR

1 cut tree shape

Choose 16 jelly roll strips from a holiday fabric collection. Select a mixture of colors and values. Cut (1) 18″ segment from each strip. Sew these together lengthwise. Press all seams to the same side.

Square up one side of the strip's ends removing all selvages.

Fold cut edge over 6″ keeping the seams straight. Angle a long ruler to create half a tree. Avoid going beyond the 11th strip. Cut along the ruler's edge.

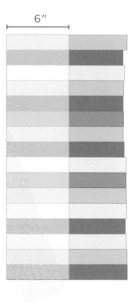

1 cut tree shape from fabric

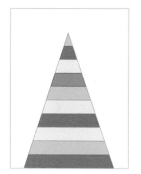

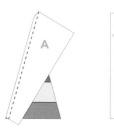

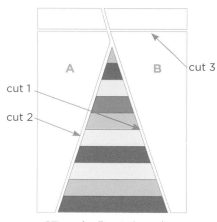

2A background yardage: sides straightened, fold removed

2B make 3 cuts in order

3 attach background A & B; make 2

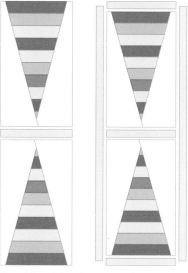

4 add sashing between the 2 trees; add borders next

Yield: 4 setting triangles: 2x A & B

To make the second tree use the first one as a template. This time open the "fabric" and cut along both sides of the first tree.

2 background

With the background yardage folded just as it comes off the bolt, square up both raw edge sides and remove the fold at the bottom. **2A**

Lay a tree on the bottom edge, centering it on the fabric. The first cut will extend off the fabric above the tree's top. The second stops at the tree top. Make a third cut horizontally 1" above the top of the tree. Make sure it is perpendicular to the sides. **2B**

3 sew

Attach section **A** to the left of the tree first, then **B** to the right side. Make sure to match the small end of the triangle with the large bottom of the tree, right sides together (RST). Press to the background. Make 2. Square up both tree sections so they are the same size.

4 sashing & border

Remove selvages from the **BBB** fabric & cut (6) 2½″ x LOF (54″) strips. Set 3 aside. Subcut 3 sections the same width as the tree unit. Attach 1 between the two trees. The tree points are oriented toward each other. Always press to the sashings & borders. Attach the last 2 sections to either ends of the runner.

Measure the length of the runner. Subcut (2) sections to that length. Attach to either side. Press toward the borders.

The remaining **BBB** fabric (approx. 26″ x 54″) is the backing. Sandwich the runner on batting and backing. Quilt as you'd like.

5 bind

Square up the runner. For binding use the (3) 2½″ x LOF strips that were set aside. Sew together with diagonal seams end-to-end. Trim; press seams open. Fold in half lengthwise WST and press. Attach to the runner's edge. Finish by hand or by machine. *See pages 100-101 for more detail about attaching binding to the quilt.*

For the tutorial and everything you need to make this quilt visit: **www.msqc.co/ quiltedchristmastree**

LET THE

Spirit

OF **LOVE**

fill your

HEARTS & HOMES

this holiday

SEASON

Merry Christmas + Happy New Year

LOVE, THE DOAN FAMILY

all wrapped up

QUILT SIZE
61" X 81"

DESIGNED BY
Jenny Doan

PIECED BY
Kelly McKenzie

QUILTED BY
Cassie Martin

QUILT TOP
2 packs 5" holiday fabrics
    (2x each print per pack) **OR** (1)
    10" square pack holiday fabrics
1¾ yds sashing solid
1¼ yds outer border
(4) ¼ yd cuts for ribbon & bows

BINDING
⅝ yd coordinating fabric

BACKING
5 yds coordinating fabric
    OR 2 yds 90" wide

SAMPLE QUILT
Bumble by Tula Pink for Free Spirit
Fabrics
Designer Solids - Gray by Free
Spirit Fabrics

ONLINE TUTORIALS
msqc.co/allwrappedup

QUILTING
Loops & Swirls

QUILT PATTERN
pg 64

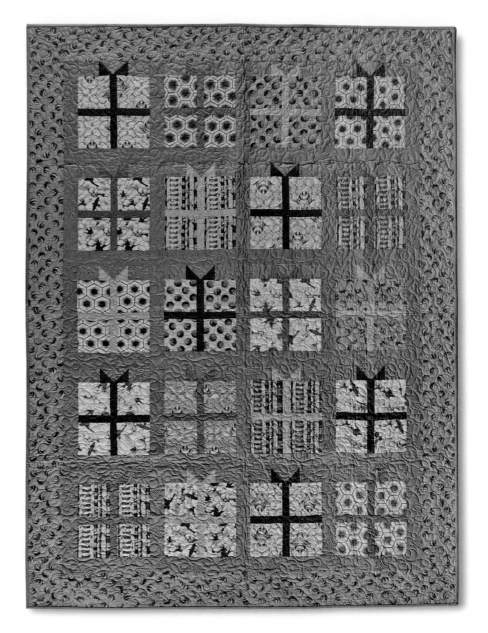

 TIP: *Want to make a different size? No problem, check out these and other patterns online!*

charmed spools

QUILT SIZE
58½" X 63"

DESIGNED BY
Jenny Doan

PIECED BY
Kelly McKenzie

QUILTED BY
Sandi Gaunce

QUILT TOP
(1) 5" square pack
¾ yd spool fabric solid
1¾ yds background/inner border solid
1 yd outer border

BINDING
½ yd coordinating fabric

BACKING
3¾ yds coordinating fabric

SAMPLE QUILT
Caswell County by Jo Morton for Andover
Cotton Supreme Solids: Doll Face (067) by RJR
Burlap Solids: Clay by Benartex

ONLINE TUTORIALS
msqc.co/charmedspool

QUILTING
Spools of Thread

PATTERN
pg 8

dala horse

RUNNER SIZE
17½" X 40"

DESIGNED BY
Jenny Doan

PIECED BY
Jenny Doan

QUILTED BY
Cassie Martin

PROJECT MATERIALS
(6) 10" squares **OR**
(6) 5" x 10" rectangles
from scraps
½ yd outer border

SASHING/BINDING/BACKING
1½ yds coordinating fabric **OR**
different fabrics option:
¼ yd sashing,
¼ yd binding &
1½ yds backing

OTHER MATERIALS
12" x 12" square of red felt for
appliqué **OR** 12" x 12" square of
cotton fabric + Pellon Fusible
interfacing
freezer paper for tracing
OR Sizzix Die #659074
glue stick optional

SAMPLE RUNNER
Snow Days by Mitzi Powers
for Benartex

ONLINE TUTORIAL
msqc.co/dalahorse

QUILTING
Stipple

PATTERN
pg 40

dresden placemats

PROJECT SIZE
(4) 23" X 15" placemats

DESIGNED BY
Natalie Earnheart

PIECED BY
Kelly McKenzie

QUILTED BY
Mary Bontrager

MATERIALS
2 packs of 5" squares
½ yd solid background

BINDING
¾ yd coordinating fabric

BACKING
1½ yds coordinating fabric
  cut into (4) 27" x 20"
rectangles

SAMPLE QUILT
Downton Abbey: Lady Rose
by Kathy Hall for Andover
Fabrics

Bella Solids Silver (187)
by Moda Fabrics

ONLINE TUTORIALS
msqc.co/dresdenplacemats

QUILTING
Stipple

QUILT PATTERN
pg 72

foil-topped ornaments

PROJECT SIZE
6" - 8"

DESIGNED BY
Jenny Doan

PIECED BY
Kelly McKenzie

PROJECT MATERIALS
2½" WOF strips
Fusible fleece
Aluminum foil 12" wide
Heat n' Bond

OTHER TOOLS
Easy Cut Circle Ruler
18mm rotary cutter

SAMPLE ORNAMENTS
Holiday Flourish by Peggy Toole
for Robert Kaufman

ONLINE TUTORIALS
msqc.co/foilornament

QUILT PATTERN
PG 32

94

hexagon ornament runner

PROJECT SIZE
19¼" x 37½"

DESIGNED BY
Jenny Doan

PIECED BY
Jenny Doan

QUILTED BY
Cassie Martin

MATERIALS
MSQC 10" Hexagon Template
10" square Pellon Fusible interfacing
¼ yd tiny black rick-rack for hangers
(6) 10" squares
¼ yd background/inner border
⅓ yd outer border

BINDING
¼ yd

BACKING
¾ yd coordinating fabric

SAMPLE QUILT
Rudolph by Quilting Treasures
Cotton Supreme Solids Optical White (033) by RJR

ONLINE TUTORIALS
msqc.co/hexornamentrunner

QUILTING
Stipple

PATTERN
PG 56

it's all an illusion

QUILT SIZE
67" X 94"

DESIGNED BY
Jenny Doan

PIECED BY
Kelly McKenzie

QUILTED BY
Cassie Martin

QUILT TOP
1 pack 10" squares
1½ yds shadow solid
2¼ yds background solid

BINDING
¾ yd coordinating fabric

BACKING
5¾ yds coordinating fabric

SAMPLE QUILT
Artisan Batiks by Lunn Studios
for Robert Kaufman
Kona Cotton White & **Gray** by
Robert Kaufman

ONLINE TUTORIALS
msqc.co/illusion

QUILTING
Loops & Swirls

QUILT PATTERN
PG 48

missouri star

QUILT SIZE
75" X 98"

DESIGNED BY
Natalie Earnheart

PIECED BY
Natalie Earnheart

QUILTED BY
Emma Jensen

QUILT TOP
1 print pack 10" squares
4 yds background solid
¾ yd outer border

BINDING
¾ yd coordinating fabric

BACKING
6 yds coordinating fabric

SAMPLE QUILT
Prisma Dyes
by Artisan Batiks for Robert Kaufman
Kona Cotton White (1387)
by Robert Kaufman

ONLINE TUTORIALS
msqc.co/missouristar

QUILTING
Loops & Swirls

QUILT PATTERN
PG 16

 TIP: *Want to make a different size? No problem, check out these and other patterns online!*

patchwork stocking

STOCKING SIZE
12″ X 17″

DESIGNED BY
Jenny Doan

PIECED BY
Natalie Earnheart

QUILTED BY
Natalie Earnheart

MATERIALS
(1) 5″ square pack
     makes 4 stockings

BACKING, LINING, CUFF
½ yd fabric for each stocking
OR 8″ x 16½″—cuff
     (2) 14″ x 18″—lining & backing

SAMPLE QUILT
Evergreen
by Kim Schaefer for Andover

ONLINE TUTORIALS
msqc.co/patchworkstocking

QUILT PATTERN
PG 24

two table toppers

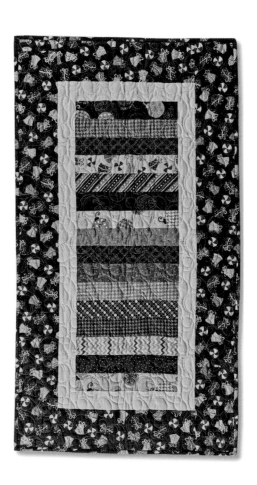

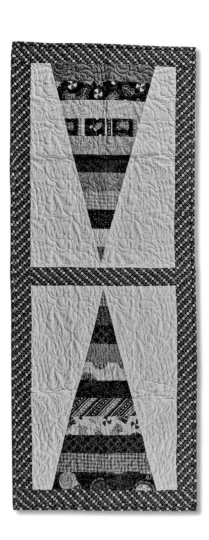

CANDYLAND RUNNER
23½" x 44"

QUILTED CHRISTMAS TREE
18" x 47"

DESIGNED BY
Jenny Doan

PIECED BY
Natalie Earnheart

QUILTED BY
Sam Earnheart
Lauren Dorton

CANDYLAND RUNNER MATERIALS
(1) 2½" WOF print roll
¼ yd inner border
½ yd outer border

BACKING & BINDING
1½ yd coordinating fabric

QUILTED CHRISTMAS TREE MATERIALS
(1) 2½" WOF print roll
½ yd background solid *(or use same roll as above)*

BORDER, BACKING & BINDING
1½ yds coordinating fabric

SAMPLE QUILTS
Merry & Bright by Kimberbell Designs for Maywood Studios

Cotton Supreme Solids Optical White (033) by RJR

ONLINE TUTORIALS
msqc.co/candylandrunner
msqc.co/quiltedchristmastree

QUILTING
Jingle Bells
Pine Tree Meander

QUILT PATTERN
pg 80

general guidelines

- All seams are ¼" inch unless directions specify differently.

- Cutting instructions are given at the point when cutting is required.

- Precuts are not prewashed; therefore do not prewash other fabrics in the project

- All strips are cut WOF

- Remove all selvages

- All yardages based on 42" WOF

ACRONYMS USED

MSQC	Missouri Star Quilt Co.
RST	right sides together
WST	wrong sides together
HST	half square triangle
WOF	width of fabric
LOF	length of fabric
QST	quarter square triangle

pre-cut glossary

CHARM PACK
1 = (42) 5" squares or ¾ yd of fabric
1 = baby
2 = crib
3 = lap
4 = twin

JELLY ROLL
1 = (40) 2½" strips cut the width of fabric
      or 2¾ yds of fabric
1 = a twin
2 = queen

LAYER CAKE
1 = (42) 10" squares of fabric: 2¾ yds total
1 = a twin
2 = queen

The terms charm pack, jelly roll, and layer cake are trademarked names that belong to Moda. Other companies use different terminology, but the sizes remain the same.

When we mention a precut, we are basing the pattern on a 40-42 count pack. Not all precuts have the same count, so be sure to check the count on your precut to make sure you have enough pieces to complete your project.

press seams

- Use a steam iron on the cotton setting.

- Iron the seam just as it was sewn RST. This "sets" the seam.

- With dark fabric on top, lift the dark fabric and press back.

- The seam allowance is pressed to the dark side. Some patterns may direct otherwise for certain situations.

- Follow pressing arrows in the diagrams when indicated.

- Press toward borders. Pieced borders may demand otherwise.

- Press diagonal seams open on binding to reduce bulk.

binding

- Use 2½" strips for binding.

- Sew strips end-to-end into one long strip with diagonal seams, aka plus sign method (next). Press seams open.

- Fold in half lengthwise WST and press.

- The entire length should equal the outside dimension of the quilt plus 15" - 20."

plus sign method

Diagonal seams are used when straight seams would add too much bulk.

- Lay one strip across the other as if to make a plus sign RST.

- Sew from top inside to bottom outside corners crossing the intersections of fabric as you sew. Trim excess to ¼" seam allowance.

- Press seam open.

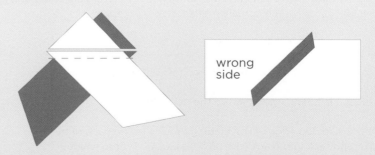

wrong side

attach binding

- Match raw edges of folded binding to the quilt top edge.
- Leave a 10" tail at the beginning.
- Use a ¼" seam allowance.
- Start in the middle of a long straight side.

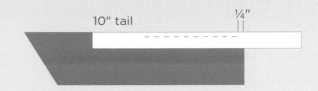

miter binding corners

- Stop sewing ¼" before the corner.
- Move the quilt out from under the pressure foot.
- Clip the threads.
- Flip the binding up at a 90° angle to the edge just sewn.
- Fold the binding down along the next side to be sewn.
- Align the fold to the edge of the quilt that was *just sewn*;
- Align raw edges to the side *to be sewn*.
- Begin sewing on the fold.

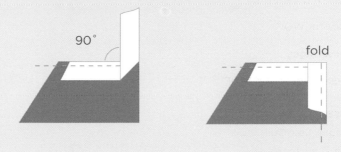

close binding

MSQC recommends **The Binding Tool** *from TQM Products to finish binding perfectly every time.*

- Stop sewing when you have 12" left to reach the start.
- Where the binding tails come together trim excess leaving only 2½" of overlap.
- It helps to pin or clip the quilt together at the two points where the binding starts and stops. This takes the pressure off of the binding tails while you work.
- Use the plus sign method to sew the two binding ends together, except this time when making the plus sign, match the edges. Using a pencil mark your sewing line since you won't be able to see where the corners intersect. Sew across.
- Trim off excess; press seam open.
- Fold in half WST and align all raw edges to the quilt top.
- Sew this last binding section to the quilt. Press.
- Turn the folded edge of the binding around to the back of the quilt and tack into place with an invisible stitch or machine stitch if you wish.

borders

- Always measure the quilt center 3 times before cutting borders.
- Start with the width and measure the top edge, middle and bottom.
- Folding the quilt in half is a quick way to find the middle.
- Take the average of those 3 measurements.
- Cut 2 border strips to that size.
- Attach one to the top; one to the bottom of the quilt.
- Position the border fabric on top as you sew. The feed dogs can act like rufflers. Having the border on top will prevent waviness and keep the quilt straight.
- Repeat this process for the side borders, measuring the length 3 times.
- Include the newly attached top and bottom borders in your measurements.
- Press to the borders.

PATCHWORK MURDER

PART 5
Short-arm Stitcher

——— A JENNY DOAN MYSTERY ———

written by Steve Westover

Angela Fuchia's door was secure but the room next door was open. Jenny peeked inside. A cleaning cart blocked the door and hotel staff tidied up inside. Jenny coughed loudly but the cleaning woman continued working. "Excuse me," Jenny said, finally getting the worker's attention.

The petite young woman wore a crimson apron and barely looked old enough to be out of Middle School. "Yes ma'am," she said with well-rehearsed courtesy.

Jenny channeled her high school thespian days as she played a new role. She spoke with a thick southern twang and her hands flew with wild gestures. "I'm locked out of my room and my husband has the key. Can you please help me? I'm in such a hurry."

The young woman fidgeted and then looked down at her feet, clearly nervous. "The front desk will be happy to assist you," she said. "I can't...I apologize. It's a security thing."

Jenny nodded and then stifled a cry. Her hand rose to her chest as if attempting to hold her emotions in. "I understand," she said between heaving breaths. "I'm just so late." Her accent kicked into overdrive. "I left my grandkiddys in the lobby so I could get my car keys. Those little monkeys are probably bawling something fierce. What am I going to do?" Jenny averted her eyes but monitored the cleaning woman's reaction nonetheless. Then, feigning an epiphany she wiped imaginary

tears from her eyes. "Can you call downstairs on that walkie-talkie thangy you have there?" The name is Angela Fuchia. Please, I just need in for a minute."

The woman looked as if she'd return to her cleaning but then she hesitated.

"Please," Jenny repeated.

The woman's expression contorted into a pained expression while she thought but then strode briskly around the cart, out the door and stood in front of room 220. "Just for you, ma'am."

"Well aren't you the sweetest thang," Jenny said. "I am going to tell that nice manager lady how much you helped me and how much I appreciate your kindness."

The cleaning woman held up a defensive hand. "Don't mention it. Your appreciation is all the reward I need."

"Bless your heart," Jenny said and then stepped inside.

Jenny closed the door and stood with her back against it as she surveyed the room. The bed was made and a hard, silver suitcase lay on top. Jenny looked at the nightstand, the desk, and the entertainment center but all were free of clutter. She hurried to the bed and unlatched the suitcase not knowing exactly what she was looking for. Jenny felt uncomfortable rummaging but convinced herself it was for Angela's own good. She latched the case closed and then opened a slender compartment on the front. Inside she found a quarter inch file which she slid out and spread across the bed.

Jenny glanced over a patent application and a signed sales contract and then at diagrams for a short-arm stitcher. The stitcher was no larger than an average sized sewing machine but instead of a control console where a user would select and run a limited number of design patterns it was controlled only via a smart phone app. Like industrial quilters this short-arm version would simulate the sewing path before stitching ever began to ensure precision. Jenny had heard rumors of attempts to upgrade stitcher functionality with smart phone technology but she hadn't seen any that lived up to the hype.

She fumbled through a stack of papers but paused when she found a high gloss customer brochure. Not only was this new stitcher model ready for sale but the price stunned her. She held the paper close to her face as if refusing to believe. $1399.00 for the base model was very affordable and the app priced at $59.99 with multiple add-ons priced at $14.99 each was a steal.

Jenny found herself getting excited to own one herself. Reading more about the app that controlled machine operations Jenny was even more impressed by the custom design features it boasted. Each new add-on to the app would provide new quilting designs for quilt lovers everywhere. If the brochure proved to be a truthful representation of the product Jenny knew it would be an overnight sensation with hobby quilters around the country. The new stitcher would instantly challenge popular machines by established companies.

The pieces of the mystery came together in Jenny's mind the same way a new quilt design sometimes would in her dreams. Jenny took a deep breath as a wisp of fear brushed against her. The stakes were high and the apparent corporate espionage had already proven fatal for Bruno. Pulling the papers back into a stack Jenny prepared to place them into the front compartment of the case. She stopped. If the murderer was still looking, which he surely was, she couldn't make it easy for him to find.

Lifting the hotel mattress Jenny prepared to slide the file underneath but she paused again. Too simple, she thought. Then rushing to the closet Jenny removed a plastic laundry bag and slipped the file inside. She pressed out all the air and tied the top of the bag into a tight knot before moving quickly into the bathroom. She removed the lid from the toilet tank and set the plastic bag in the water. She replaced the lid and then hurried from the room.

Jenny wondered what kind of trouble she might get into. She had entered a room that wasn't hers, though technically she hadn't broken in. She had removed property from a luggage case, but she hadn't actually taken it. She had simply secured it. She wasn't sure if her justifications would satisfy law enforcement but she was confident she had done the right thing for Angela. One thing was certain…it was time to get Detective Scanlan involved. She needed to tell him everything she knew.

***

Jenny smiled sweetly at Detective Scanlan but her eyes glared. "You did what?"

"I followed you," Scanlan repeated as a matter of fact as they both climbed onto the elevator. "I watched you and that nice old lady talking. Then she went to the desk and back to you. I knew something was up."

"You got all of that from me speaking to a fellow quilter?" Jenny asked.

Scanlan shrugged. "I'm a detective. I detect."

Jenny sighed but as much as it pained her to admit it, Scanlan's presence saved her the work and time of searching for him. In her mind she organized what she knew.

"Is there something you'd like to tell me?" Scanlan asked. Jenny bit her lip and grinned. "I have some information I'd like to trade you." She let her statement sink in for a moment and then continued. "I'm happy to share if you'll provide me the same courtesy?"

Scanlan's eyes narrowed as he attempted to evaluate the woman he had previously underestimated. "Yes," he said with a slow nod. "But you first."

The words raced from Jenny's mouth as she explained how she had tracked down the name of Angela Fuchia as another passenger on the airport shuttle from the night before. Then her words slowed as she considered how to describe her entry into Angela's room. "Ah, forget it," she said setting aside her caution, worried more about finding the killer and protecting Angela than protecting herself from Scanlan. Jenny described the contract, the patent application, and plans for the personalized stitcher and apps, sharing her assessment of the value of this new product in the quilting market.

Detective Scanlan listened intently as Jenny shared her theory of corporate espionage as a motive for murder. In simplest terms it was a robbery gone bad. "There is seldom honor among thieves," she reminded him. "Bruno had attempted to retrieve the plans for the stitcher but failed when Angela's luggage was lost by the airline. Since Bruno offered nothing of value the murderer disposed of him to tie up loose ends." Jenny smiled proudly.

Scanlan folded his arms. He appeared unconvinced.

"The killer must not have expected Bruno's body to be found so quickly," Jenny added. "But he must be aware now because of the police presence. He may be getting desperate. We need to find him fast." Jenny paused so Scanlan could share what he knew but the detective appeared to be deep in thought. "Your turn," Jenny prodded.

Scanlan nodded thoughtfully but Jenny could see uncertainty in his lively blue eyes. "I've had hotel security keeping an eye on the few men attending the conference. There are only seven so it's not hard."

"Do any fit the description MK gave you?"

Scanlan shook his head. "No. But he may be in disguise."

"Disguise? So we need to find Angela Fuchia before he gets to her," Jenny said.

"Agreed."

Detective Scanlan spoke into his phone while he and Jenny hurried through the lobby towards the Columbia room. Sitting at their usual table, Betty and Mary Ann greeted the duo as they approached. "You have less than an hour until your presentation," Betty said cheerfully. She reached under her table and held up a bag. She quickly unzipped it to reveal a hideous plaid housecoat. "I told you I'd find you something to wear."

Jenny's eyes widened at the sight of the housecoat but Scanlan's nearly popped. "You're very kind," Jenny said. "But I'm still in the middle of something."

"Don't worry. I'll save it for you right here," Betty said. "Did you find Angela?"

"No," Jenny said. "Do you know where she is?"
Betty looked at Mary Ann, questioning. Mary Ann responded.

"Of course. Follow me."

Scanlan ended his call and placed his phone into a front jacket pocket while he waited for Mary Ann to stand. Betty had been slow but Mary Ann had her beat. They all anxiously waited while Mary Ann grabbed her walker from beside the wall.

Inside the Columbia room vendors and suppliers lined the walls. They stood in front of tables or in booths aimed at drawing excited quilters their direction. Mary Ann pointed diagonally across the bustling room. "She's over there. The Treudeau booth."

Jenny and Scanlan looked at each other. "She may be in danger," Jenny said. Scanlan nodded. Not waiting for Mary Ann to keep up, Scanlan and Jenny pushed through the crowd to find Angela Fuchia.